PILLOW PRINCESSES & TOUCH-ME-NOTS

*Fuck You! Stonefemmes and Stonebutches
are Taking These Terms Back!*

By Victoria Anne Darling

PILLOW PRINCESSES & TOUCH-ME-NOTS

Fuck You! Stonefemmes and Stonebutches

are Taking These Terms Back!

DARLING PUBLICATIONS, INC.

This book is for every one of us, forged by pressure.

Our brilliant Stones, diamonds, lesbian outliers,
and boundaryless ex-pats.

May we never be melted again,
unless it be on our terms and our timing.

ACKNOWLEDGEMENTS

The first person I need to acknowledge is Jo Woolnough. Jo, this book is thanks to your strong and steady presence in my life, where you quickly created a harbor for me as my editor. You have been one of my most valued resources. Badassery, personified.

No monumental undertaking, and this book, likely the single most important one I will ever produce, would have never made the journey had it not been for Melissa Kreutner. I *love* knowing that my community has you, a warm, vibrant, heterosexual woman to thank for the insights that will shift and bless their lives. Love comes from all sides when you are open to it, and I know I can speak for my community's collective "we" when I say, it was your love that mattered most.

Blass Ingame, you are by far my favorite Blasstard, and your intellectual insights helped me develop this content in ways you are not aware. Thank you for challenging us all to think. We are better for it. Yes, even if you do not give a fuck. The world needs more mxters, gentlethems, theydies, and folx like you.

Marti Schneider, the inimitable Big Bad Daddy Stone, your friendship and support of this book – the long calls reading through sections of early drafts, transcribing my garbly-gook, and cheering me on when I was tired and almost faltered – thank you for holding the Stone light so I could see.

Nicole Bracknell, I am grateful for your brilliance, personal and Stone allyship, friendship, and savvy spiritualness. You have been fun to get to know as we giggle with a candle under the covers trying not to set our hair on fire, scheming for better lives.

Jessica and Daphne Chilton. Our paths no longer cross but I would be sorely remiss not to mention how the two of you and your intelligence, bravery, and humor helped me grow my theories for this book. Your presence is missed, though I am certain you are both being watched over by everything good.

Corvus and Alexis Genco. I recognize your journey is filled with learnings and explorations of all manner of other things, but the idea of this book was fueled by you both. May your lamps always have oil and your bed more heat than your animals can stand.

Robin Gordon (waving to the uber beautiful Tabatha in the background). Your voice has always been that of powerful queerdom, social justice, and keen intellectual goodness in a way that continuously reminds me to stand in the shoes of inclusion at every turn. You are one of my favorite heroes.

CR Ritchey. Our community is so fortunate you exist within it. You show us every day that no matter what our circumstances or the challenges we face, there is still time to be who you always wanted to be. You are a Stone warrior.

Shane Whalley. You inspire me. I admire the single-focus dedication you have committed to: that of bringing grace, nuance, and clarity to the inherent racism, class and racial inequalities, and gender/sexuality/identity/ability biases we all carry within us. If folx have not seen you teach or speak, they are sorely missing out. You are one of the genuinely great ones.

Mare Melton. I still recall all our many calls discussing the nuances of our beloved Stone community. You are one of our warriors and protectors. May you and the beautiful woman who has captured your heart live in Stone harmony for a lifetime.

Kay Patton. Kay, you gave me friendship and a safe harbor during a challenging few weeks and I have never forgotten your kindnesses. May it all come back to bless you a thousand-fold. Your music and keen mind deserve to be here. We need you.

Xan Toler-Santos. You have always been such a bright spot in my life. I adore your glitter unicorn gloriousness and believe that Marilyn Monroe never had a better example of her va-va-voom.

Stone for Stone (Butch/Femme). If you have never been a part of this Facebook group, you have sorely missed out. Many of you helped me grow and certainly contributed to some wonderful, rich conversations. Thank you for letting me see you.

***

There can be no acknowledgements for the language of Stones if not for Leslie Feinberg. Leslie, wherever your form now exists, thank you for plotting the course that allowed me/us to follow your footsteps. Without your brave, introspective work, and the commitment you showed in distributing your much-needed words, we would have circled in the wilderness much, much longer than we did. Because of you, we are building home.

TABLE OF CONTENTS

PART I: WHO THIS IS FOR

INTENDED AUDIENCE

I am writing this for the butches who always wanted to be fully masculine but never received the right encouragement.

For the butch who died inside and closed off another piece of their interior landscape because a touch boundary was disrespected or seemed too difficult to convey.

I write this for the butch who believes that dating ultra-feminine, straight, cis women is the only way to ensure their body is touched correctly.

I write this for the femme or butch, whose new romantic interest has shared that they have a stone identity and want to explore its meaning to understand their partner better.

I write this for the partners of stonebutches and touch-me-nots, who feel relief when they learn they do not have to touch female genitalia in return for their own pleasure. I also write this for those who love stonebutches and touch-me-nots but are confused about navigating the seemingly many boundaries that best suit these bodies.

I also write this for the femme, aroused by the heightened vulnerability achieved when there is no reciprocity expected during sex, including mutual nudity.

I write this for the femme who blossoms and moves into deep wells of giving whenever she is the *only* sexual recipient during their intimate exchanges.

I write this for the femme who was never allowed the erotic desire to *not* touch her partners in the same ways that she enjoys receiving touch.

If you know you are different than other lesbians, this book may be for you.

If you are female identified but enjoy dressing entirely masculine and prefer only sexual intimacies that support a masculine experience of your body, this book is for you.

If you are male identified in your mannerisms, sexuality, and thinking, but know you do not want to transition to male, you need to read this book.

If you are a femme who has been called greedy or selfish because you have little interest in traditional "lesbian" sex acts, this book may help you understand yourself better.

If you are a femme who loves and respects male-identified butches who are also *non*-male, this book will make for a stimulating, insightful read.

If you are a femme that worships the masculinity of butches and wilts in disappointment when one of them suddenly reveals a feminine side – you absolutely *must* read this book.

If you teach or hope to teach women's studies, you need this book too, because the minds of your students, whether they fall into one of the groups of individuals discussed in this book or not, will need to be made aware of them. They also need to understand the inherent feminism in *choosing* boundaries, particularly sexual or touch ones, even when those boundaries are outside societal norms.

My intention is only this: to define and illustrate these terms –
pillow princesses, touch-me-nots, stonebutch, and stonefemme
– for masculine of center (MOC) and feminine of center (FOC)
lesbians, and those who love them.

PART II: INTO DAYLIGHT

FACING THE RISKS

I am sitting in a cabin with my laptop perched on my knees, in a town so small there are no salons, no bookstores to browse, and no antiquing (unless you call piles of rusted front-yard junk melting into the earth, a picker's paradise). There is only one restaurant, which is open for breakfast three days a week and dinner on Fridays – except when the church has a fish fry and everyone goes up there, forcing the diner to leave the closed sign up.

It is quiet here. Every road is painfully, deeply rutted. There is no enforcement for unleashed animals, overgrown grass, or midnight-construction-crews dumping onto empty plots of land. You either grow up here and can't afford to move away, come here to get away from city life, or to stop here for just a bit so you can look inward or pull something out of yourself, without distraction.

I fall into the last category. I opened a map and picked what appeared to be the most remote spot I could find, a full three-hour drive to the nearest hub of civility. I came here to spend dedicated time writing, to finish a book – *this* book – which had been a concept for more than a dozen years. But I could never get past the introduction. Hell, I could not get past the first half of the intro. I had tons of notes, invested plenty of time deciding the layout and artistic feel, and worked, and reworked the few pages I had, several times. I simply could not gain traction on producing the meat of the damn thing.

Until I figured out why.

My hold-up was not due to fear of success. Or fear of failure. Nor was it: writer's block, procrastination, or failure to launch syndrome. I did not lack inspiration or motivation either, as lord only knows I have had plenty of those – because how else would I have plodded along this long.

It was the terror brought on by my feelings of codependency, plain and simple. The throat-seizing fear of rubbing someone the wrong way. So much so that the body shuts down and action is limited to preserving life.

As if I would die, had I proceeded with my writing.

The terror was about you, dear reader. Worry that you will misunderstand what I need to say; misunderstand what so many people of a certain type need to hear.

This is a controversial book, and as it is with any first step into new terrain, there is potential it will offend someone or a group of someones.

Without any existing materials to address these topics, the first educational book out of the gate about Stones is bound to be wildly misunderstood. It may even create divisive arguments within the community that I am writing about.

I have decided to break through those fears.

PART III: WHY THIS BOOK

THE COST OF CLOSETS

I saw my first tomboy when I was five. I was inside my maternal grandmother's large nursery school, running past a large bay of windows that overlooked the courtyard playground when I saw her.

She was alone and seemed the same age as me. She climbed up a heavyweight slide, the metal shiny and heated from the summer sun, and rode it down with a furrowed brow. She then climbed back up, before riding back down, repeating the series again and again. I noticed how contained she seemed. Never looking up or around as other kids might have, wondering where everyone else was. She appeared lost in thought. Comfortable and uncomfortable, simultaneously. As if entertaining herself seemed old habit.

I stopped in my tracks, watching her, my mouth hanging open, for what felt like an eternity. Not because she was strange, but because we were unrecognizably similar. I, a tow-headed daddy's girl who favored wearing my satin *"I Dream of Jeannie"* outfit, as I bopped my head, with its high ponytail, to grant wishes. She, wearing a boy's denim, long-sleeved shirt, and matching dungarees, her dark unruly locks, and scuffed white sports shoes setting off the perfect frame. Nothing about us matched, yet everything did. I felt in her what I had in me, yet I had no language (in my late 1960's preschooler's mind) that explained what I had experienced. It was the first magical experience I had, and I did not quite know what to do, except stare.

31

I recall instantly wanting to be her wife. To kiss her face all over when she was sad, to pirouette in front of her to show off my newest ballet routine or tutu, to have her look at me in awe and wonder when I gave her our first child. To save her from the harshness I knew must lie ahead. To shelter her in storms.

I wanted to say, *I understand*, and *Me too.*

But what was it I "got," exactly? And where did such an enchanted creature come from? Were there more? How could I find them? What did this mean about me?

Suddenly, my world made sense. A sense of understanding passed over me, then. A desire I had no words for, but that managed to alter my direction, completely. *No wonder* I hated touching and being touched by little boys when we played doctor. *No wonder* I resisted being paired with a boy as a designated husband when my friends and I played house. I wanted *her* to be my husband. I wanted *her* to touch me.

Unfortunately, I was just then pulled away for a dance class, and when it was finished, I ran through the entirety of the building looking for her. But she was gone, never to return.

I looked for her, or someone like her, for the next twenty-plus years.

Almost instantly I began to hold back in my engagements with girls my age when the subject of role-playing our favorite movie stars came up. I silently wondered if any of them were like me. Different. Not wanting a 'him' for a husband, but rather a her-him. I had no other word that made sense. I simply knew my truth.

But I also knew, I needed to hide it.

There was no way I could have understood the cost of hiding this knowledge, from those around me, or from myself. Every time my grandmother pointed out of the car window and said, "There's a queer, don't be like that," I tucked my truth farther inward. When my best friend held a necklace over my inner wrist to see if it swung left-to-right to prove I was straight, I jerked my hand away, hiding the pink of my cheeks when it swung about in circles.

I could no longer afford to play games unless I knew the rules, first.

Yet, as difficult as those moments were, they were just the precursor to something inevitable and larger.

Years later, when my grandmother caught me "playing" under the covers with a tomboy friend, she told us to get up and follow her downstairs. There had been no way to hide the fact that my pants were down as I did what I was told. The slew of horrifying and damnation-laden comments that projected out of her mouth, directly at me, when she discovered my transgression, was enough to have me seal my real self away, forever.

At that moment, I was welded shut. I divorced my true desires and began to learn how to be something else. *Someone* else.

I spent decades being anyone other than myself, successfully denying my true self. This meant I no longer had access to my innate sense of right and wrong. Being someone other than my true self also required leaving behind my intuition because the stepping outside of myself no longer gave me access to it or confused my trust in it. This "stepping away" and masking the person I was intended to be also required losing the connection to my gifts and talents, and, sadly, my dreams.

I was consumed with figuring out who I needed to be to survive, because my authentic self could not help me avoid experiencing more of the horrors I had already endured.

When you are not loved and nurtured into who you were born to be you lose not only yourself, you lose *everything* that self comes with. And, for every year you stay disconnected, the number of years required to regain yourself grows.

During those lost years I was able to make connections, form relationships, and experience love, but I did not have the internal compass needed to direct my growth within these relationships. I had learned as a child to project what was expected and approved, without any idea of how to project the real me, after having spent so many years actively hiding my true self.

Living a life without being authentic is confusing and hard to track. I felt as if every day, a new version arose, one that was even harder to know than the previous me. The relationships I had during this time were destructive. I attempted to promise someone something, but then had no idea how to deliver on that promise; how to love them, how to provide things that I *should* have been able to provide. I was also not receiving things I genuinely wanted. Why? The problem is, if you cannot look at yourself authentically, then you cannot see someone else authentically, either.

This loss happens to many people, the whole world over, every day, when they are influenced by parents, caregivers, lovers, friends, or teachers to be someone they are not. Someone those others *wish* them to be. Someone more to their liking; less gay, less out, less biologically attracted to the "wrong" gender, and/or less drawn to behaviors, ways of dressing, or ways of being that are unacceptable to these influencers.

Unfortunately, shifting to accommodate the influences and preferences of these others, always results in lost years filled with mismatched and devastating relationships, and unrealized talents and dreams. These losses tremendously affect every person that fails to receive the encouragement to discover who they were meant to be. But, especially those, who are directed away from their innate sexuality.

This book focuses on lifting the veil for a very specific group, to help these unique and fascinating individuals sift through the maelstrom of possibilities, to find a shared experience, common language, and a chance at real, lasting happiness – maybe for the first time, ever.

Stone Butch Blues, by Leslie Feinberg, was our first insight into the lives of stonebutches – many of whom identified as touch-me-nots. Their feminine lesbian partners, now referred to as pillow princesses or stonefemmes, were only nominally mentioned. None of which were adequately explained.

My two previous books, *A Stone's Throw*, and *A Stone Shelter* provide insight into my personal articulation of who we are and how some of us love. They feature essays, poems, and characters, both real and imagined, and, though helpful, even they are limited in their exposition of what we are.

Once you can understand and articulate who you are, you can begin to understand your body's urges and a more accurate draw towards a mate that is wired for you, exactly as you are. This allows you to know that you have a legitimate place in this world, and a community, waiting for you. That, friends, is when everything shifts.

It is literally a life-altering perspective.

You can begin unpacking shame. You can gain the power to make better choices. You can *choose* the options you never saw before.

You can learn to celebrate *you*.

Whether that 'you' is a high femme, low femme, hard butch, soft butch, genderqueer, third gender, Two-Spirit, enby (nonbinary), or any of so many other gender presentation types, here we celebrate you.

Purpose

This book aims to provide an understanding of our terminology. It gives insights into the lived contexts of these individuals. It provides recognition for these authentic sexualities, to encourage empowerment and self-esteem. Most importantly, this book aims to create distinctions that reinforce healthy boundaries, through validation and recognition.

This is important to me because our community has been rife with physical, emotional, and social-level violations due to tightly held misunderstandings and not knowing we (and our boundaries) are valid and deserve to be celebrated.

This book will help you see you are not alone, that there are not only others out there like you, but that there are those who want *only* you, *as* you. It will help you see your potential happy ending; of what comes when you engage with those who get you, want you, and are exactly like you.

Truly compatible partners and well-informed, encouraging friends are everything.

Throughout this book, you may gain an understanding of where and how the chemistry starts between two Stones. The mental and emotional navigation that takes place, in order to make space for our intense, passionate sexual expressions.

You will also learn how to set better boundaries, recognize boundary violations and violators quicker, and – even more importantly – you will be better armed to extract yourself from uncomfortable and unhealthy situations.

This is the book you have been waiting for. This is the flashlight in the world that has had only confusing darkness.

This is the moment *you*, finally, get to shine.

And, in shining, you get to attract those that *really* get you.

PART IV: DEFINITIONS

JARGON

Within these pages, you will see me use two terms for specific groups of femmes: pillow princesses and stonefemmes. I will also use two terms for butches: touch-me-nots and stonebutches. The terms for femmes will often be interchangeable, as will the terms for butches, except when we are speaking of their differences: pillow princesses and touch-me-nots do not ever have contexts where their touch limits shift or have flexibility. They simply are what they are. Stonebutch and stonefemme boundaries can sometimes have specific ways or contexts that certain kinds of touch are allowed with the right partner when the requisite levels of trust have been achieved. (See the Definitions section for more information on the differences.)

I would also like to state that I am pointedly using stonebutch and stonefemme as one word each, instead of "stone butch" and "stone femme." The reason for this is because all manner of other people, including heterosexual men, have begun to use "stone" to describe their desire to be the pleaser, preferring not to receive sexual touch.

While I can appreciate someone's desire to develop self-determined language to communicate who they are, "stonebutch" and "stonefemme" mean so much more than the boundaries they convey. We are a people, a community. We have a long and storied past that we have had to struggle to earn and carve out. Anyone else using the term stone stands on our shoulders. So, I invite you to own our Stone history. Own our hard-won lives and truths. Use our single-word identifiers with pride to tell the world we, a people, exist, and that our sexualities are not adjectives. We are nouns. We are Stones.

HEADSPACE

The idea of headspace will be addressed in more detail further into the book, but I think it's important to note here that the way each person mentally processes their desire for their partner, is a crucial element of the Stone dance. Just as touch-me-nots and stonebutches see or experience their expressions as masculine and/or male within sexual encounters, stonefemmes and pillow princesses desire to see and experience their partners in those same ways too.

Mindset − "seeing" someone as they wish to be seen rather than focusing on the literalness of their biological parts − is a way of reinforcing the delicious contrasting masculinity/femininity that is at the core of these special unions.

The stonebutch and touch-me-not need to know that their partner sees and experiences their masculinity, and sexual expressions of that masculinity, as real and legitimate, equal to or better than any other masculine person on the planet. If the partner doesn't, then that stonebutch or touch-me-not must not only carry their own experience of their masculinity alone, they also have to cross the legitimacy bridge on behalf of their partner as well. When their partner carries a similar headspace as their own − about their partner's legitimate masculinity -- then the stonebutch and touch-me-not can let go of the extra head noise and simply relax into their desired experience of themselves.

Likewise, pillow princesses and stonefemmes need, not only the same in return – supporting and celebrating their experience of their femininity – but they also desire a masculine partner who celebrates and lives fully into their masculinity, especially in sexual exchanges. If someone is uncertain of their partner's masculinity or is not affirming of the pillow princess or stonefemme femininity, then the pillow princess or stonefemme must not only support their own need for those things but cross the divide for their partner in their mind, also.

The good news is that maintaining your headspace for your masculinity or femininity is easy, once you embrace it.

PILLOW PRINCESSES

The Flower

Pillow princesses, starfish, or do-me-queens – take your pick – they all have a bad rap. These derogatory nicknames conjure up images of bored, lazy, and selfish women who refuse to move out of the missionary position during sex, arms and legs spread wide, waiting for lovers to service them without any reciprocity, pleasure, or sexual satisfaction in return whatsoever.

Who, in their ever-loving, right mind, would want *that*?

These women have a reputation as the worst sexual partners. Lesbians especially, but most people in general, ridicule this type of lover for being self-absorbed, entirely uninterested, and not at all engaging, in the lovemaking department.

Other descriptors include: "passive sexual recipient," "dysfunctional," or simply those with "heteronormative obsessions." Some people even assume these individuals are a product of old traumas.

Beyond asking who would be interested in performing sexual acts on a 'dead-fish' so to speak, I am instead requesting you to consider that maybe, just maybe, there *is* someone yearning for this type of partner.

Someone who aches for a femme who loves to completely surrender her flesh to curious hands, who opens her body, psyche, and sexual energy for another to come and drink from, until they are quenched.

Could it be that these women live to give their body to a partner, who in turn, live to give pleasure without receiving physical touch in return? I know without a doubt, there is.

This receiver is someone so incredibly well versed in nuances, that they give more than you could imagine, even with no "apparent" exchange.

Their reactions, such as an arched back from feeling the gentle touch of a hand guiding her, is giving; the careful but firm digging of her nails into the muscles of her partner is also giving; a woman who, in every moment, breath, and remark, validates the masculinity that envelopes their lover, gives.

Isn't the passive well, its only task to provide fresh water to drink, a much-cherished gift to the thirsty drinker?

What if a sexual recipient embraces her vulnerability – and finds it erotic to stay in that space? Is that the act of a selfish, bored, or lazy person?

What if a pillow princess suspends her issues surrounding self-esteem, shyness, and worry in order to open herself fully, despite being denied equal vulnerability – or the distraction of focusing on her partner's body in return?

What if she experiences a measure of fearlessness, beyond any she has known before, simply by being willing to strip away all her inner guards in order to let pleasure, and orgasms, be "taken" from her?

What if she opens herself in this way, and it creates a sacred space, a place for her partner to surround themselves in energy and in a sanctuary that connects them both - to something akin to the Divine?

What if this pillow princess has decided, consciously, to give her body up as a healing tool, for all the times her partner's boundaries had been violated? What if this choice occurs simultaneously; her, owning all her sexual agency in ways no one has ever allowed her to before, while seeming to be completely submissive?

If this is what we knew about these women, would we still consider them a cold, impartial lover?

Would we still think of them as self-absorbed takers?

Pause here for just a moment to consider this...

Could pillow princesses be the primary givers?

Even when her partner centers all their sexual energy on her?

A giver could be a baker, toiling with love, over the selection of the best ingredients and patiently hovering near the oven to ensure the batch does not burn, removing them at just that perfect moment. But the giver might also be the person who buys cookies to donate to a fundraising table, or the person, who every year, devours their friend's gift of cookies, that they do not even like.

Conversely, a "taker" is someone we have been socialized to believe does not care for anyone, save their own self and interests. A taker is considered one of the worst of all human beings; a person that consumes more than their fair share, someone who is filled with greed and selfishness; someone whose ego is out of control and through that, they thoughtlessly create imbalance wherever they go by taking more than what is offered, more than they should, and/or in a way that diminishes the giver.

But can't a taker also be a giver?

What about someone, like a death doula, who agrees to bear witness during the final stages of someone's life – "taking" onto themselves the dying person's fears and loneliness, offering in its place, ease and comfort in their final moments.

Or the Tibetan Buddhist practice, called Tonglen, whereby the practitioner "takes" on the suffering of others to restore compassion and reduce their own karmic debt.

These examples of taking have giving at their core. It entirely depends on the context.

This other side of taking, where at its core, is an act of giving. The pillow princess 'gives' through her surrender; her active role in vulnerability is vital to what the perceived 'taker' – the stonebutch – requires to be fully satisfied. She is a woman who allows a touch-me-not to take all the pleasure from her body that they want. A woman, who stands in the nude before her fully dressed partner, allowing herself to be fully seen without the safety of reciprocity. She is a woman who knows that she may never see her partner in the same state, never touch them in the same manner.

That is bravery.

That is *giving*.

Pillow princesses – which I have dubbed touch-THEM-nots – are courageous adventurers of intimacy, accepting and celebrating their touch-ME-not partners exactly as they are. They understand the touch-me-not's boundaries and find those boundaries both intensely erotic and infinitely exhilarating.

The pillow princess is turned on by experiencing vulnerability, objectification, and worship. The more intense the vulnerability, the hotter, as long as it is kept in balance with respect and appreciation for who they are and what they are giving.

Exposed

In approximately 370 BC, a woman named Phryne was born in Greece and had many famous suitors and benefactors who held positions on the city council. When she incurred capital charges for being a courtesan, she was brought by her jailer to face the council. Just as she was losing the case her jailer abruptly ripped off all her robes, exposing her nude body to everyone present. I imagine her standing there, shoulders squared, exposed, ready to face any judgment.

It is said that her physical beauty is what tipped the scales in her favor, but a beautiful woman who recoils, suddenly stripped in shame or embarrassment, is not a compelling image. It is a woman – of any physical style or level of beauty – that accepts and embraces the piercing and invasive gaze of others at her most vulnerable, that generates the greatest degree of awe and appreciation. Exhibiting your innermost vulnerabilities shows a strength of character that is often jaw-dropping.

It is said that her beauty caused the council to dismiss all charges. Standing in front of those that *could* judge her, knowing they reveal nothing to her in return, is a potent power imbalance; the power in her ability to stand stripped of protection is raw, intense, and moving. It conveys agency over oneself, and a level of fearlessness few ever attain.

Pillow princesses and stonefemmes might be the bravest of all femmes. The ones who have dominion over their own sense of self – so much so, that the judgment of others, even *as* they are vulnerable, matters so little they have no need to cover themselves.

These women offer this expression of strength to their masculine partners.

They offer vulnerability as a gift to contrast their partner's masculine power.

Each of these women stands fearful *and* fearless in her nudity so that she can experience the greatest degree of power in her vulnerability. To feel it coursing through her, to them.

This act makes her a vessel for their pleasure. Her vulnerability feeds her partner's experience of power. She is her partner's vehicle, an object to be used for pleasure, in a way that creates soaring freedom in herself.

Stonefemme

The difference between a femme and a stonefemme is both minute and gigantic. Each of these women appears feminine and delights in the power in her femininity. But the stonefemme may do femininity as performance knowing that her presentation and sensuality, when accentuated, celebrated, and expanded upon, expands the permissions for stonebutches to embrace their masculinity. The more feminine the stonefemme allows herself to be, the more permission her partner gains to explore their masculinity.

As mentioned before, I use "stonefemme" interchangeably with "pillow princess," but they are not entirely interchangeable. A pillow princess is a touch-them-not, while a stonefemme *might* have more flexibility regarding reciprocal touching, done in specific ways. Both stonefemmes and pillow princesses have touch boundaries, but what those boundaries entail are what begins to differentiate them more completely.

Concave Sexuality

In addition to having touch boundaries, both the stonefemme and pillow princess are also the receivers, sexually speaking. Stonefemmes and pillow princesses are the recipients of penetration, whether literal or figurative/energetically; their sexuality is based on allowing their partner entry, in whatever manner they mutually desire. Both have a concave sexuality, in that, they are complete receivers for the lover whose sexuality is outwardly focused. Whether they do their receiving as a submissive, dominant, or in an equal exchange with their lover. The way they receive, or are penetrated, is simply an extension of their complete identity.

Seduction

Another area where these two femmes begin to differentiate is in their manner of seduction. The pillow princess does not drive initiation, directly. She often chooses a partner who prefers to initiate all sexual exchanges and determines what degree of nonsexual touch the encounter will include, while she instead focuses on giving her partner whatever they seek from her body.

Alternatively, the stonefemme may be a true touch-them-not, or, she may also be an active seducer, remaining the sole sexual recipient but also dazzling her partner with a lap dance that she initiates, or bantering and flirting saucily to ignite the sexual energy – possibly coming right out and stating what she wants and how she wants it to the partner that delights in such things.

A stonefemme might also identify as a fulltime submissive or a dominant. If she is a submissive there may be little discernable difference between her and a pillow princess, save for the rare flexibility in her boundaries outlined briefly below. If she is dominant, she will want to control how and when the sex occurs but will *only* do so within her own touch boundaries and the touch boundaries of her partner.

Touch

The flexibility of the stonefemme's touch boundaries should not be interpreted as fluid. They do not shift and alter with the wind. They are based on trust, context, and the level of intimacy achieved or offered – and all within the perimeters of how safe she feels in that moment, that day, or the context, which may or may not even relate to her partner, or how far they have come in their relationship together.

As mentioned before, some stonefemmes will not touch a partner below the waist or anywhere near their chest. Others will touch a strap-on with their hand; many will give their partner's strap-on a blowjob while being worn; a few others will provide their partner with under-strap oral, if it too, mimics a masculine blowjob. The common theme is that stonefemmes do not want to have sex in any way that "womanizes" or feminizes their partner's body.

The pillow princess adores the masculinity of her mate; the stonefemme is the same but also feels de-feminized if she feminizes her partner in the way she touches that partner. She will do what she does within the context of affirming her partner's masculinity, so anything that reminds her partner of "breasts" (rather than chest) or of more traditional lesbian sex, such as penetrating her partner or performing clitoral and labia-loving cunnilingus, also reminds *her*, the stonefemme, of the sameness of their biology, rather than the contrasting differences she loves.

AFAB Partners

The stonefemme and pillow princess do not want the illusion of being with a male, they want to delight in their erotic attraction to masculine non-males. They are not in denial. They are not pretending. They do not see themselves as straight or acting out a heterosexual fantasy. They are not female avoidant. They are not relinquishing their feminism. They are not afraid of touching female genitalia nor do they reject the odor of female genitalia. And they are certainly not so jealous of other females that they need to masculinize a partner so they can be the only feminine body in the bed.

Pillow princesses and stonefemmes both, relish the contrast of their partner's masculinity to their femininity. They may or may not be a high femme or glamour femme, those wildly feminine creatures who often adore stilettos and elegant or racy lingerie, they may instead be the stunningly beautiful Chapstick or blue jean femmes in Birkenstocks or sneakers that also delights in the contrast of their masculine counterparts.

Let me say it again: You need not be high femme to be a stonefemme or a pillow princess.

Just as the touch-me-not and stonebutch prefer a masculine self-perception, the pillow princess and stonefemme prefer a feminine one. Typically, the more masculine and feminine each respective partner is, the more accentuated and hotter that contrast is for them. Anything that diminishes that contrast, such as asking a stonefemme to wear the strap-on or suggesting the stonebutch wear lingerie, robs them of the power and sense of orientation each need, to feel whole and right. It undermines the foundation of trust they have built or want to build. It removes their clarity of which direction is their true north.

"Seeing"

The headspace of these femmes is a fascinating thing to consider.

The pillow princesses and stonefemmes of the world experience themselves as women, and they are attracted sexually, romantically, and emotionally to masculine, female-bodied individuals. Those masculine female-bodied persons may have a variety of gender identities, but what most have in common is the desire to experience their bodies, and sexual experiences, along the same lines that traditionally masculine people do. To expand the depths of these attractions, some unique mindsets have developed to support them.

As stonefemmes and pillow princesses mature and come to recognize the comfort levels and needs of their partners, they learn *not* to see aspects and features of their partner's genitalia, body style, mannerisms, and sexual accouterment (i.e. strap-on), especially when it is not worn. The reason for this is that any misdirected focus yanks the touch-me-not or stonebutch out of their masculine self-perception. It reminds their partner of the times they have been judged and mistreated or forced to endure feminizing experiences. It is also invasive; akin to peering into an area of their partner's biological privacy where they do not want undue or uninvited attention.

As mentioned before, these women are not afraid of the femaleness of their masculine partner, they simply have a sense of sacredness around it. They wish to be the one person in the world their masculine counterpart never has to fear. The one person who will never, *ever* try to dismantle the masculinity they both love. The one person who will never, *ever* feminize them. The one person with whom they will always be safe, in this regard.

Touch-Them-Not

True pillow princesses have their own touch boundaries; they are touch-*them*-nots. Her ability to engage in these moments, to find intimacy within these constraints, is because she knows herself, can communicate who she is and can accept touch limits, knowing her own intimately, also.

The cornerstone of healthy relationships and saying "yes" to interpersonal dynamics is based on an equal and opposite freedom to say "no." Choice is the bedrock of personal agency;

it is the foundation of feminism. Why would it *always* be okay to say, 'yes I will touch you' when it is not equally okay to say "no, I get more turned on by *not* touching you.'

There should never be an expectation of touch, particularly by a woman whose sexuality is wired erotically around *not* touching their partner, whether physically or sexually. If that is not your ideal sexual scenario, then you are simply a poorly matched mate for the pillow princess or stonefemme with these touch boundaries. Fortunately, there are many touch-me-not butches and stonebutches willing to step up and happily take your place.

Double Standard

In addition to the mutual double standard mentioned immediately above, the touch-me-not or stonebutch will also often not undress at all or at least entirely during intimate encounters. This is a boundary usually erected after learning about themselves and learning what they are comfortable with. Through this self-understanding, they can communicate what they need, and want, as well as their touch limits, more completely.

Fortunately, this only adds to the heat for stonefemmes and pillow princesses.

Validity

After reading this chapter you should be able to see the most important point of all: Stonefemmes and pillow princesses are unique and fully formed identities separate and apart from any partner. They do not exist because they date stonebutches or touch-me-nots, they exist because they have a sexuality based on their own unique needs, limits, desires, and sense of themselves.

Just as pillow princess does not mean cold fish, stonefemme does not mean "I date stonebutches."

TOUCH-ME-NOTS

The Bee

Each time a woman notices the shape of their butch's breasts the butch is usually mentally directed away from their masculine identity and reminded that they are female. Each time a woman looks at their butch's harness instead of looking at its silicon attachment with sexual hunger, the butch is mentally disconnected from the experience of having a real cock and reminded they are not biologically equipped the way they feel. When women "see" and mentally register female aspects of their touch-me-not or stonebutch partner's body, the butch is divorced from the masculinity that is their source of erotic heat and sexual power.

Stonebutches and touch-me-nots are not currently (or historically) supported as children, to embrace and integrate their masculinity. They are/were typically given dolls, instead of the trucks they asked for, and often are/were told to wear dresses and frilly attire to church or weddings and funerals. Most of them were also told by lesbians – many of whom they were attracted to – that they *should* want to be touched and that penetrating them was only fair because their partner had received it, so turnabout was the appropriate thing to do.

The creation of a safe headspace, of a mental working that allows the stonebutch to operate in masculine roles, at least intimately, is vital. If not for this innate understanding between both partners, the ability to acknowledge without being explicit in doing so, the magic could not begin. Two people, sharing and creating, with an instinctive understanding of the others' mental space is special. The cost of _not_ acknowledging, believing in, and living in this shared space is not only insulting, but harmful; instantly the needed safe space is jeopardized by the person thought they could trust implicitly.

Touch

A touch-me-not is a person who doesn't want to be touched in certain ways because it misgenders them, triggers feelings of a sexuality that doesn't support their sense of self or, in some other way, triggers feelings of vulnerability or violation of their personal space. The person might want to be touched in some ways but not in others. They may want to be touched sexually sometimes, and other days, not at all. There can be a road map that always works or no map at all. Depending on how they feel immediately preceding that moment, depending on what happened in their life that day, depending on how comfortable they are in their headspace and their body — any number of factors can influence how much, or whether they want to be touched.

We can start with the basics. Touch of arms and shoulders and face and hands may be okay but for some, they may not be. Others are okay if you touch them anywhere, as long as it is always done in a way that supports their experience of a masculine or male headspace. A masculine headspace is not necessarily internally male-identified; it is just a strong, powerful kind of traditional masculinity. They may still identify as female. So, they would not consider it a male headspace, they would consider it a masculine female headspace.

Others may want to express their sexuality as a male. Remember, sexual identity, gender identity and sex/gender assignment are all different aspects of a unique person. On the topic of transition, there are many factors that influence a person's choice. Age, medical history, family, profession, legalities in their region, or any number of other reasons will influence their consideration of or decision to transition, in full or in part, to male, and all of them should be supported.

Cock-Identified

Some touch-me-nots are cock-identified. For most, this means that their physical experience during sex centers around an expulsion of energy from their groin and, with or without the use of a phallic object, experience what many consider a 'male' orgasm. Others consider their tongue to be an expression of a cock, to the point that their tongue wants to penetrate; with *it* reacting strongly to sexual excitement (tightening, hardening, or tingling). For others still, the expression of their sex is through their hand; they want to penetrate and use their fingers, palms, and fists to stimulate all parts of a woman. The hand, in this sense, acts as their phallic object and the center point of their ejaculating energy.

Penetrative Sexuality

What most touch-me-nots and stonebutches have in common is that they have a "penetrative" sexuality, an outwardly focused sexuality; they want to *get in there*, they want to feel the feminine partner open up for them, they want to have her release outwardly and they use her body to release *their* energy into her and out of her through her orgasm.

Alternatively, the pillow princess and the stonefemme are concave sexualities. They are recipients, even if they are on top or dominant; their body is the vessel for what is penetrated by a hand, a finger, a phallic object, or tongue.

AFAB Resolution

Stonebutches and touch-me-nots do not want to be acknowledged as feminine. That means that showing womanliness, girlishness, or being called princesses, queen, ladies, etc. does not work for them. Likewise, they do not want their bodies to be seen as feminine. They may identify as female. They may prefer she/her pronouns. They may be mothers and have a different experience of their body, and their emotional relationship with it, when they are with their child. They maybe feel as if they are the daughter to their mother but, outside of those sorts of specific contexts, and in a sexual experience of their body, they typically all want to feel that they rest in the masculine end of the spectrum, presentation-wise and physically.

Some touch-me-nots are non-binary (enby) and love the experience of not trapping their bodies, and perception of their bodies, on a binary scale. In this respect, while they may still have touch boundaries and specific needs, sexually, their gender expression may be more fluid, given the timing and tone of a moment.

The ones that do want the experience of feeling masculine, typically do not like having breasts. Regardless of size, most dislike and even hate having female-like attention given to their chests. Having their nipples, or breasts touched in any way can easily emasculate them and removes them from the comfortable headspace of having a masculine "chest."

There is a lot that a partner can do to support that headspace by not "seeing" their partner's body as feminine or female. Respect could be shown by avoiding statements like, "Wow! Those are curvy hips." Or "Wow, you really have a rack on you." Or worse, "Wow, bring those boobs over here and let me motorboat them." As a stonefemme, that may be as horrific for me, as for my butch. Because I want to support their experience of having a masculine relationship with their body. I want them to feel powerful and safe and sexy. To do that, the easiest way is to focus instead, on the length of their muscles or the size of their arms or the quad muscles in their legs, or how broad and powerful their back is; things that will help them remember that they are a masculine entity to me. And in the world.

Erotic Contrasts

One of the things that almost all touch-me-nots and pillow princesses really love is the experience of contrasts in their gendering. Their hyper-femininity juxtaposed to a partner's hyper-masculinity. Some of the individuals in these unions fall more toward the middle of the scale, masculine just of center or feminine just of center, with no an extreme in either direction. Yet, the contrast between them accentuates their experience of power. Stonefemmes and pillow princesses experience their power through femininity, and stonebutches and touch-me-nots experience theirs through their masculinity.

The Myth

There is a lot of speculation about why a touch-me-not does not want to be touched. Some like to think that it is based on abuse. If they had not been violated as children, then they would not need such strong boundaries. That is a bunch of hogwash. Lots of folks have been completely violated and do *not* have the touch-me-not boundaries. Still, others have *never* been violated and have complete and utter anti-touch boundaries. The two are not related. There are times it is true, but for the most part, it is not.

Bur here is the real kicker. Abuse and trauma cannot <u>create</u> eroticism or orgasms for whatever is opposite of the abuse. So, let us resolve that, permanently, right here and right now.

Abuse of your gender expression can <u>never</u> cause you to be sexually turned on by anyone you are not organically attracted to in a physical and pheromonal. If a touch-me-not were created as a result of trauma or damage, how on earth could that make them sexually aroused by partners who prefer their unique sexual wiring, restrictive sexual and physical boundaries and the adoption of more than their fair share of vulnerability? It is just not possible.

Setting boundaries for yourself does not have to be a push against what occurred in the past. It can just be a positive choice for yourself that supports your headspace, your relationship with your body, and your experience of being powerful in the world.

Sometimes, no-touch boundaries occur because someone's body is hypersensitive. There is a phenomenon called a Highly

Sensitive Person (HSP), and there are some books written about it that are really good. It can simply be a person who is extremely sensitive to touch, so what might feel like a light touch to you makes them want to scream and crawl out of their skin. It may be physical or emotional hypersensitivity, or it could just be that they feel more grounded and centered when they are not having to fend off the touch of others, and process the energy that their body collects as a result.

Butch Versus Stonebutch

A butch is a masculine person assigned female at birth (AFAB) that may or may not be a stone; may or may not be a touch-me-not; may or may not be female-identified; may or may not be non-binary identified; may or may not be masculine-identified. A butch may feel like they are feminine in bed and masculine in their presentation or some combination thereof, but the difference between butch and stonebutch is that a stonebutch has specific genital touch boundaries that the non-stone butch does not.

The non-stone butch will often like reciprocal sex. Meaning they might want to be penetrated by their partner, they might want to receive un-restricted oral, they might want any number of things that a stonebutch or a touch-me-not does not want. That is usually the dividing line between the two.

A stonebutch may enjoy oral stimulation genitally, especially if it simulates a masculine blowjob on their clit (a.k.a. "other cock"), but not all do. (Nor do all stonefemmes offer this.)

Stonebutch Versus Touch-Me-Not

The difference between a touch-me-not and a stonebutch is a little more refined and nuanced.

A stonebutch may have touch boundaries but still like to receive attention on their bodies. That attention may be, kisses on their forearms or kisses on their belly, and/or kisses on their strap-on. It may be occasional for some, but not for all for others. It may be occasionally a partner's mouth under their strap. As mentioned above, some may want that oral under the strap to mimic a male blowjob, so the clit becomes the other cock.

Some stonebutches may imagine their vaginal opening as a place to stimulate their testes or consider it a prostate in their minds' eye, and, as long as their partner can mimic the way that testes or a prostate may be stimulated and language like "vagina" or "clit" are not used, the stonebutch is not thrown from their headspace. They can relax and enjoy it. These persons are not common, but they do exist.

A touch-me-not is *not* going want touch under a strap and sometimes they will not even want touch *on* their strapped cock, or they may not want *any* touch below the waist, even on their hips. Additionally, some will not want any touch on their chest, even if it is done in a masculine way. Others will be okay with nails in the back or strokes on their arms, and others want absolute control and have absolutely no desire to deal with any of that. They instead focus the entirety of their sexuality on their partner. They might restrain their partner by holding her hands down, or they might like a little bondage so that there is absolutely no question about whether they will be touched, ensuring they are the sole driver during sex.

Often the more masculine the butch, the more feminine the femme feels and vice versa. It is the love of contrasts that draws and nourishes their attraction to each other, and that includes how they sexualize and limit or extend touch.

Female- Versus Male-Identified

Some will be exclusively female-identified and still be a touch-me-not or a stonebutch. Some will be exclusively male identified. Others will vacillate between the two depending on the context, the day, the person, or their headspace. And still, others may be queer-identified, neither female or male, or they might be non-binary identified, possibly meaning not queer, not male, not female or some blend of each. All of those are legitimate. Often, but not always, stonebutches and touch-me-nots are cock-identified, meaning that their strap-on, or the experience of their body in the genital region, can come with an explicit kind of focus.

So, a butch that does not wear a strap-on for physical limitation reasons, for financial reasons, or for comfort reasons may still consider their groin a 'cock.' For some, it is too intense to think about strapping, the shame wrapped around it is too much, or they cannot cross the psychological divide and go into that headspace. Yet that region of their body still feels like it has a cock, even if it is invisible; they may use their body by thrusting their hips against the femme partners' buttocks or via tribadism (scissoring between the legs); it may be that they use the femme's face to rub against, it can be any number of ways and still feel like a cock to them inside their head. Other butches are not cock-identified – they are oral identified. They do not want to have anything to do with a cock because they do not relate to one at all, or they see it as accouterment like a toy to put on at times, to round out the festivities, but it is not actually the way they see their body.

A cock-identified person has a cock, whether it is there, strapped on, or not. And, they particularly appreciate having a partner who thinks and feels that way, too. It is imperative, for this dynamic to be flawless, for the femme to take in the realness of a cock-identified butch.

PART V: INTIMACY

ORGASMS & SEX

There are many types of orgasms. Some orgasms occur in specific areas for anyone assigned female at birth. Others occur mentally. And others experience orgasms with their whole body. Some require direct clitoral stimulation (or "other cock"), some people can orgasm without being touched at all, and still, others can have a climax simply from stimulation of their vaginal orifice, their G spot, their rectum, breast, inner thigh, being whispered to, etc. Some of them experience their orgasms as an outward explosion, a mental explosion, or an internal explosion.

These can be true for stonebutches, touch-me-nots, pillow princesses, and stonefemmes, equally.

A stonebutch or a touch-me-not can have an orgasm through the orgasm of their partner. So, their partners' orgasm becomes crucial to their pleasure because that is *their* experience of release as well.

There is also a joy that can be found in sex that does not include orgasms. Stonebutch or touch-me-nots might want to pursue sex with a woman, focusing entirely on making her climax, giving their partner a feeling of release, without an actual, physical orgasm for themselves. The sense of completion, the sense of euphoria, the sense of cortisol levels going down, the influx of endorphins; all of it can still be there without the actual physicality of an orgasm occurring within their body.

Likewise, the pillow princess and the stonefemme can have a non-orgasm sense of release or fulfillment without orgasming because she is getting off on taking on the vulnerability for her partner. Being a vessel for their pleasure and being used for their sexual excitement and relief her only goal – not because she is self-sacrificing or some sort of stone-labeled martyr, but rather because being that vessel IS her greatest source of pleasure.

Sometimes the ability to orgasm is interrupted. That can be true for all humans, not just these. So, it could be that there is life or some sort of chemical or hormonal changes going on, it could be that there is an emotional healing cycle in place, and the grief is just over large. Depression can affect orgasms, as can a lack of trust, but that does not mean that the person does not want to have sex. Sometimes they still want to provide for the needs of their partner or experience the connection that the acts of sex bring.

See this article for more info on the value of sex without orgasms: https://www.shape.com/lifestyle/sex-and-love/8-benefits-sex-have-nothing-do-orgasm.

VULNERABILITY

Vulnerability is the quality or state of being exposed to the potential of being attacked or harmed.

A lot of what you have read so far falls into the definition of being vulnerable. The creation of, and connection over, a performed, cherished ritual based on what each person develops in their headspace is a tenuous gift. The ways in which this can be attacked and exposed to harm are plenty, so genuine recognition and respect of touch boundaries and the desires each party expresses are vital. The vulnerability cultivated is subject to social pressures that prefer it not be authentic; we, Stones, are exposed to a shame many of us carry because of others' discomfort. Therefore, the (mutual) trust that is required here is crucial to our emotional and sexual health and mental wellbeing.

When pillow princesses or stone femmes take on vulnerability, they do so for both parties, and it is extraordinarily intimate for two people to allow an imbalance of power. When a pillow princess opens herself up to be touched without a reciprocal touch in return, she is in the physical receiver mode, even if that receiving is offered as a sacred gift. The physical receiver is always more vulnerable than the physical giver or the doer. That vulnerability is something that the touch-me-not or stonebutch drinks in. They feel filled by the power of the dynamic where they are drinking from their partners' energy as she "gives up her energy to be used as an intoxicant" and power accelerant for her partner.

When we speak of the vulnerable sides of these two identities, it is important to recognize that the hyper-expression of feminine and masculine is a vital part of the desire-exchange. Accentuated femininity *is* vulnerable, even if it is an expression of power. Accentuated masculinity in an AFAB person is *also* vulnerable, even when it feeds the power of the masculine person. The masculine person is saying, "I'm stepping out to take a risk here in being my full masculine self and I want you to allow me the space within and on you to do that, sexually." The feminine partner says in response, "I will allow you to express yourself into and through me, receiving your energy fully, while I exist within my most feminine and vulnerable states. Drink from me for our mutual pleasure. I am open."

It cannot be stated clearly enough though. Vulnerability, within our stone dance, is sacred.

If a stonebutch or touch-me-not has desires to be touched, sexually, or in any manner that might be considered feminizing, without clearly communicating those desires prior to sex, then that breaches this trust and violates the vulnerable space the stonefemme or pillow princess offers.

In the same way, if a femme looks to demasculinize, or touch, a person with firm no-touch boundaries, then that violates the space that was cultivated for them.

We must work to protect both sides of our stone dance: the pillow princess and stonefemme who offer up their bodies, and the stonebutch and touch-me-not who accept the risks inherent in penetrating them.

Power as Vulnerability

It may not seem logical on the surface but, consider this. The stonefemme takes on the expressions of vulnerability for both parties. The touch-me-not then moves into a position of what we perceive to be, complete power.

That perception is wrong.

The stonebutch's vulnerability is externalized by their pillow princess's vulnerability. Imagine, then, if the femme in this scene judges their partner for doing that or rejects them outright, entirely? That puts the bottom, the recipient, who we thought was more vulnerable, in the position of power. She is accepting and validating their dance by showing complete vulnerability for both of them. So, it makes this a very odd little loop that is very sexual, sexy, and rarely talked about.

The hidden, never-talked-about superpower of the pillow princess and stonefemme is the vast power it requires to take on all the vulnerability in the stone dance. Is this why so many stonebutches and touch-me-nots are drawn so powerfully to femmes who express power in other areas of their lives? I tend to think it is a secret, unacknowledged beacon that says, 'this one might be strong enough.'

Conversely, pillow princesses and stonefemmes are more often drawn to those masculine butches who are often the most rigid about not relinquishing power or delving into overt expressions or experiences of vulnerability so that they, finally, get the opportunity to test the limits of their strength for their partner.

***

There is a downside when vulnerability exchanges slip, though.

When a pillow princess or stonefemme does not take on the vulnerability for her partner, the partner's energy eventually begins to wane; over time they are not as stabilized and their powers shifts into a weakened form; they don't feel as strong, they don't feel as powerful, they don't feel as certain, so, it has a toppling effect.

Likewise, if the feminine partner is forced to give up more vulnerability than she is capable of, then she is being stripped of her power and her ability to consent and she is prevented from the ability to take on the vulnerability. It is a catch 22.

It should be noted that there are ways that too much vulnerability can be a bad thing. When a femme takes on all the vulnerability the effect can be quite intoxicating for both parties. That is a good thing, right? Maybe. Maybe not.

Unless the individuals involved are emotionally mature and self-aware there is the real possibility that too much stone dance magic can inflate the ego of the driver, whether stonebutch or touch-me-not, and ignite unexamined and unintended vulnerability in the part of the driven, either the pillow princess or the stonefemme.

A stonefemme or pillow princess who has craved all her life to be the sole bearer of vulnerability in her intimate encounters may find the successful experience of it so sweepingly intoxicating that she overlooks red flags in her partner or begins to become overly vulnerable in other areas, such as parenting or financial control.

Similarly, a stonebutch or touch-me-not who achieves the race-car champion's high, from successfully dumping all the vulnerability on their partner who devours it and even asks for more, is so filled with their sense of power and rightness in the world that they demand more than they should, assume things they should not, and might even lash out if she begins to set limits.

Care must be taken when entering the arena of feasts, especially after such long journeys of starvation. There is the danger of gorging and not recognizing when pacing is required or called for.

***

Vulnerability *can* be a deliberately shared or revered arena.

When the pillow princess or stonefemme undergoes something traumatic or experiences an extreme illness, the touch-me-not or stonebutch *can* offer to take on the vulnerability for their partner as a way to – *very* temporarily – restore their partner's sense of justice or rightness in the world. This might look like the stonebutch taking one step back in silence when the femme's emotions are running high and inviting her to expel the energy of her frustration. It might be that the touch-me-not, who usually refuses to touch *anything* feminine, places one pair of the femme's finest heels in the touch-me-not's closet so that the femme can feel fueled by intruding in sacred space that is typically forbidden. Or the touch-me-not allows their femme to touch their arm in ways that would be forbidden on other days.

The idea is that the sacrifices do not undermine the sacred trust around who is masculine or feminine or breach the sexual touch boundaries in place. Yet, they temporarily give things not usually within their comfort zone offered as a restorative tonic.

SANCTUARY/HARBOR

A sanctuary is a well-known concept that describes a place where someone can seek solace, a place of refuge or safety. Pillow princesses and stonefemmes typically consider themselves to be a sanctuary, a place where their partner can come to find respite and worship. A place to visit and receive nourishment. A place to come and find restoration. To feel whole again. To re-center oneself. To gain resources. To realign. To be right in the world and right in your body. A place to go inside and be fully affirmed for all that you are. Too often stonebutches and touch-me-nots do not get that in the world, so pillow princesses and stonefemmes offer the only sanctuary their partner may ever know.

A harbor is very much like a sanctuary, but it is a place of protection from rough waters, a home, a shelter, a place to weigh anchor and rest. It, too, is a place that provides refuge, but it does it in a protective way rather than a directly nurturing one. It contains needed resources, but it does not typically spoon feed them to you and wipe your brow. It is a shield, a barrier to the outside elements, whereas the sanctuary is the source of life.

A pillow princess and a stonefemme will each reject any expression of masculinity in themselves. This includes wearing the strap-on during sex. It might include taking the lead role sexually, (though they might do that from a feminine perspective, such as a lap dancer, a coquettish vixen, a seductress, a goddess to be worshipped, etc.) The expressions of masculinity that they reject might be taking out the trash, changing the oil or a tire, mowing the lawn, or other "traditional" versions of activities considered masculine.

Pillow princesses and stonefemmes want to experience the heat and the power that comes from being hyper-feminized, though that does not always look the same for each woman. One might want the hyper-feminine version of long glittery pointy nails and feather boas and another might want to wear Birkenstocks, a knitted scarf, and the Chapstick that makes her feel feminine.

The pillow princess and the stonefemme feminize themselves for power. Sometimes they feminize themselves for softness or in the rejection of power, such as a girl who is more of a wallflower and shy, wanting to be drawn out. Some will take on the hyper-femininity in motherliness, as a nurturer who cooks and dotes on others, preferring to take care of them. She might embrace her hyper-femininity as an edgy biker, fire dancer, or sex worker, or someone who revels in the fierceness and the intensity of her edges, in their unique and femininely powerful way. They might do it in more traditional relationships or they might do it in kinky ones where they are expressing these things as a slave or submissive, consensually, of course.

***

We are taught that touch is a natural, everyday part of living. You shake hands with strangers. You hug people even when you do not know them. You are supposed to sit on Santa's lap when you go to shopping mall. There are a thousand ways that we have culturized touch without giving anyone the freedom to say, "that's too much for me, I am more sensitive to touch," or "I feel vulnerable in a way that I'm not comfortable with."

We are taught that others do not, necessarily, listen to us, with respect to our boundaries. That fact shapes our perceptions, teaching us to give and receive touch, without examining how we feel about the level of touch, or what our boundaries might be. This norm tells us subconsciously that we need to ignore limits.

We need to pay attention to what is important to us. We need to consider why social norms are more important than our personal identity and our personal sense of what is right and wrong for us. We are taught that our vulnerability, when we are on Santa's lap or when we are hugged by a stranger, is theirs, to be given on demand, or should be ignored altogether. We are taught that if we do not want to hug, too bad; the message we receive is that our boundaries and our limits are unimportant or secondary to what is more socially acceptable: touch.

This has created all kinds of trouble. Allowing others to interpret and define what touch is good and normal is a negative vulnerability.

The appreciation for, and recognition of, boundaries between the pillow princess and stonefemme with their stonebutch or touch-me-not counterparts then shows how touch can be interpreted differently. The limitations highlight how we both see touch as sacred, filled with nuance and meaning and provides the *opportunity* for pleasure, but also the opportunity for violation. The dedication to looking for cues in their partners regarding what is and is not okay is admirable. The work both stones do to understand their own boundaries and the effort they undertake to learn to follow that in themselves is why this relationship is so special.

DANGER

If a pillow princess does not yet know the language for her sexual wiring, and if she has not come into completely understanding her limits, trust can be damaged easily.

What if she agrees to surrender during a power-exchange, but did not fully understand the meaning of that? What if she crosses her boundaries, then? From the other side...some butch partners indicate agreement and understanding of her boundaries, but do not actually respect the strictness of them or the effort it took to create them. Or worse, when they see her boundaries as challenges to overcome.

More worse still, is when a lover believes they can accept the pillow princess's limits, but in a moment of passion – particularly when they are the dominant – they physically move this femme's body in order to receive sexual stimulation, despite her boundary of being the complete sexual receiver.

The same occurs for the stonebutch and touch-me-not all the time. Their non-stone partner does not understand or seek to respect the firmness of their touch or gender presentation boundaries, and all too often sees this partner as selfish or their boundaries as something to be overcome. Remember, no means no the *first* time, not more so after it has been screamed in anger. There should *never* be a time that an explicitly stated touch boundary is questioned after it is made clear.

Finally, there are those who believe they can accept these boundaries, but, without proper foresight (or thoughtful pause and deep consideration), they do not realize how incomplete they may feel within this dynamic. *Stones, beware.* Your partner's enthusiastic agreement never ensures commitment to your boundaries once you get to intimate moments. That kind of trust is built outside, and inside, the bedroom. NOT in promises or conversations.

Unfortunately, all of these are real examples of people I have known. Sometimes someone will call themselves stonebutch because they aspire to be "ultra-masculine" or to portray what the femme wants, rather than being who they are. These "stonebutches" simply want a hyper-masculine experience of themselves, but that does not necessarily relate to being stone.

The only way a pillow princess or stonefemme can be certain if they are making a wise partner choice is to explore what definitions each person holds for the same words, and then back that up with the careful exploration and confirmation of the person's ethics and strength of character. *Especially* how those ethics and that depth of character show up in stressful and complex situations, which takes time.

Most people consider pillow princesses to be submissive as well as the sexual bottom. While that is true in many cases, it is not true of every person or of every relationship that the pillow princess enters. You can be as dominating from the bottom as you can be from the top. A dominant can order a sexual submissive to serve her and still respect the sexual submissive's touch and sex boundaries. The two are not mutually exclusive.

BOUNDARIES

Stones are boundaried people. If there is one single thing that defines us, it is our firm development, understanding, conveyance, and delight in or celebration of our physical and sexual boundaries. It is where we get our heat from. It is the source of our power and passion. Within those boundaries, we come alive.

Because of this, we are often acutely aware of where our boundaries are not respected or acknowledged both in and out of intimacies. We may or may not have language for what we feel, but we *know* when something is not right and someone is not respecting our space or our preferences.

The more we learn about ourselves the more we begin to discover just how important feeling heard is – not just for ourselves, but hearing others, too. When we are around others of our tribe long enough, we eventually get the support we need to demand respect for our boundaries and, in return, we become hypersensitive to the respect others deserve for their boundaries, too.

And what could ever be more important than listening deeper to ourselves and others, and respecting boundaries.

Those of our own and those belonging to others.

EPILOGUE

WHAT'S NEXT

What is needed next?

We need stone-themed poetry, erotica, fiction, and biographies. We need collections of lived experiences – stories and images that capture those moments, struggles, and achievements.

We need more outness.

We need self-help books that help us achieve maturity and reclaim our lost lives. We need meaningful conversations where we talk about how our lack of stone education impacts our professional advancement and what that does for our self-esteem, social development (where we become chronic high-schoolers, even into middle age), and in our relationships, both intimate and not.

We need educators, podcasters, and social media influencers to promote these ideas to help others explore their sexuality in safe ways and gain access to peers who support and understand us.

We need to remember there are only so many stones and it is likely we will be interacting with folks again and again, so good behaviors towards those we dislike is a must, when it is possible and safe.

We need to offer each other tips on how to support one another on these topics in our public threads and how to "build" community and "call in" those who misunderstand us. (I am intentionally adopting 'in' as opposed to calling someone out, because I want us to be gentle and mindful of each other's histories and have the intention to grow cohesively as a collective.)

We need to use the topics in this book to strengthen conversations with others; to challenge the theories and points I propose so that the conversation can be taken further.

We need to continually deepen our self-examination and make space for the imperfect journey of self-awareness in others.

We need to refine our boundaries; making more space for our valid truths and adjust them only when the context, person, or experience feels right.

And letting them stand tall and proud just as they are.

WHAT WE ARE NOT

It is important when defining things, to identify what those things are not. Here we will tie up any loose questions by addressing the most common assumptions Stones face.

These assumptions include:

1. Role-players

The sexualities described within these pages do not depict people *emulating* binary genders, sexualities, or identities. Stones, the bearers of these identities, produce a traditional-looking coupling (whether heterosexual or butch/femme) but they are a unique class of people outside of these couplings that operate within specific needs, desires, and patterns of living. Stonebutches may model masculine or male mannerisms, but there is more to their erotic desire than their masculine presentation. Additionally, the expression of femininity by Stonefemmes explores a queered version of that femininity and female sexuality. What appears to be "traditional" on the surface or in the outward presentation may have truly little resemblance to what is occurring inside and between these partners.

Gender presentation (masculine or feminine) does not necessarily copy gender identity (male or female, trans, or cisgender) or reflect sexuality. These are all specific intersections within each person. No matter how well defined the masculinity or femininity of these individuals, you cannot assess or understand the celebration of the queerness within their union nor grasp how erotic that queerness is for them unless you stand in their shoes, as one of them. Marginalized individuals cannot be fully assessed or defined by an outsider.

2.   Male wannabes

Touch-me-nots and stonebutches often have strong expressions of masculinity. Whether through their presentation, mindset, or sexual activities, their masculinity is only one aspect of their experience and self-expression. Stonebutches may identify as female, others, as trans-masculine. Others feel more aligned with a third gender, as a two-spirit, as a tomboy, hijra, stud, or nonbinary (enby). Regardless of gender identity, a masculine expression may be a vein connecting all other expressions that make each one unique. For touch-me-nots and stonebutches, their mindset during sex can seem very male, and they may enjoy having their body touched and related to in a non-feminizing, or masculine way, but this does not mean they wish to transition to male, nor are they trying to copy cis-men. From most accounts, stonebutches do not want to *be* male, it is just natural for them to act in ways that align with male-identified people, as opposed to traditional female expressions of sex. Some of these MOC people *do* experience themselves as male, and have no desire to make a transition to being a male, or wish to keep their experience of being a dyke, female, or enby person is addition to feeling male, which means they are no more a "wannabe" than any cis-male.

3.   Heteronormative

Heteronormativity is a view that promotes heterosexuality as the normal or preferred sexual orientation. Outsiders confuse

Stone coupling as a mimicking of heterosexual couples because one is masculine presenting, the other, feminine. Binary cultures such as ours have a need to organize people in ways that make sense to them – in this case, on a gender binary with one person representing the 'man' and the other the 'woman.' Since this is how we are socialized, it is difficult to break from this thinking and to begin to think of ourselves in any other way.

When someone (often a non-stone lesbian) challenges me, saying that I am acting out heteronormativity based entirely on my socialization and upbringing, I recognize that they do not understand how deeply I have examined this idea for myself.

What do I really care about others' thoughts on the matter, after all? Only *I* know how much work I have put into self-reflection, deeply testing my perceptions of myself and my romantic interests and looking into the 'why' of my choices. They cannot see how many times I have exhausted myself trying to ensure I am not in denial about my motives. They cannot see how strong my sense of agency is, particularly regarding the choosing of my romantic partners. They cannot see or know how my sexual bells start ringing around the stone and touch-me-not objects of my desire, which could *never* be the result of socialization or "acting out."

The nuances conveyed between a stonefemme and a stonebutch run deep and follow a dance that is communicated through rituals unique to us, that are rarely translatable to outsiders.

    4.   Damaged

We, homosexuals, have been designated as damaged, or wrong, throughout our entire lives by heterosexuals. Our subset of female-bodied people, both stonebutches and stonefemmes, is also considered to be a damaged class, even within the lesbian community. Our desire for, navigation towards, and negotiation of stone-boundaries is not recognized or accepted outside of our tiny little Stone sub-group. The fact that stonefemmes are *turned on* by the restrictions that stonebutches have – with stonebutches reveling in the levels of giving we stonefemmes can express without reciprocal contact – goes way beyond what can be understood by outsiders, especially when bias is in the way.

Just because someone does not easily comprehend or see themselves in our paradigms and sexual preferences, does not mean they do not exist, have no value, or are in any way damaged. *We* get to self-determine what works for us. *We* get to say who we are. Until society makes space for our legitimacy as a people, only *we* can recognize good health amongst our kind.

5. Pseudo lesbian

The definition of a lesbian is a female, or woman, who has sex exclusively with another woman. The *type* of female they are attracted to does not change this qualifier. Touch-me-nots and stonebutches are female-bodied (assigned female at birth: AFAB) people, attracted to other female-bodied (AFAB) people, even if some of them do not want their genitalia touched, or, in the case of pillow princesses and stonefemmes, they are attracted to *only* masculine- or male-presenting females.

Being male-identified and non-trans does not disqualify someone from lesbianism, any more than being attracted to a male-identified-non-male does.

That said, there are many amongst our people, me included, who are uncomfortable with the term lesbian as an identifier. Does it seem "lesbian" to be attracted to the most masculine parts of my AFAB partner and desire to only treat their body in ways that underscore that masculinity? Not so much. Does it seem "lesbian-ish" for a touch-me-not to reject female-to-female centric sex acts such as scissoring and receiving cunnilingus, or for a stonebutch to want strap-on blowjobs? No, definitely not. Too, sometimes the term lesbian, when used as an identity, creates a dysphoric reminder of femaleness that diminishes the masculinity the touch-me-not or stonebutch has had to work so hard to uncover, bring to the surface, and embrace.

6. Transgender and Situational Stones

Transgender people are those who innately feel that they were born into the wrong body for their correct gender identity or expression. In the context of stone, gender and sexuality are often confused or conflated because, as a culture, we link them together. Sometimes, touch-me-nots or stonebutches decide to transition to male, but still use the descriptors that help them to help others understand their sexual wiring. This means they continue referring to themselves by their pre-transition identities. Furthermore, there are cisgender, heterosexual people such as professional dominatrixes (happy with their biological sex) who use our terms, then enjoy full physical, sexual relationships at home with their heterosexual partners, which is a "situationally stone" persona. This book does not speak to any of these outliers. It focuses exclusively on the historical definitions of touch-me-not, pillow princess, stonebutch, and stonefemme: all lesbians, not men, not part-time stones, nor heterosexuals or bisexuals.

GLOSSARY

AFAB: Assigned Female at Birth, and the counter acronym, AMAB (assigned male at birth), have been created to designate that biological sex does not preclude gender identity or expression.

Asexual: a person who does not have sexual feelings or associations.

Butch: a masculine-identified, or presenting, AFAB, who has romantic and sexual attractions to other women.

Butch Blowjob: the performance of giving the silicone dildo a blowjob that provides both the wearer and the person performing the blowjob the experience of a *real blowjob.*

Butch Cock: the headspace that validates the butch's clit, and/or their dildo, as a cock; also, the dildo, usually worn in a harness across the hips.

Cisgender: aka 'cis' or 'cissexual'. This term refers to someone whose gender matches their assigned sex at birth. This word is opposite of the word, transgender. Cis does not relate to sexual preference, instead, is solely used to indicate gender.

Cock-Identified: an AFAB who is driven, sexually, by using a cock for sex acts.

Cock: "Other": also called 'other cock.' the 'cock under the cock,' the 'under strap cock,' or 'little cock.' This is the butch clit with an expectation from one or both parties that it will be treated as if it is a biological cock.

Concave Sexuality: a sexuality that derives pleasure from receiving the insertion of something into their body, whether that be a partner's tongue, hand, or phallus.

Dominant: the position of power and control between two people who are exchanging power.

Enby: Phonetic spelling of the N and the B in "non-binary." A person who does not find their 'gender' expression on the binary scale. Unlike androgynous people (partly male, partly female in gender expression), non-binary people are not interested in being defined on the traditional binary oppositions.

Female-Identified: a person who identifies with a feminine expression of gender or sex.

Femme: a lesbian woman who embraces a feminine expression

FOC: feminine-of-center. A person who identifies on the feminine end of the gender spectrum.

Genderqueer: someone who plays with the representations of male and female, typically identifying with both male and female roles and expressions. Or a person who "queers" their typical gender expression.

Heteronormative: a worldview that promotes heterosexuality as the normal or preferred sexual orientation. Or one where you can acknowledge the seeming similarities, without agreeing that is actually the case.

Hijra: a hijra is a person whose gender identity is neither male, nor female. Based predominantly in South Asian (especially India) cultures, this person is typically AMAB and dresses as a woman. It can also denote a person who is transgender, or in the process of transitioning.

Male-Identified: a person who identifies with a male expression of gender. Does not require a desire to transition to male or become a transman.

MOC: masculine-of-center. A person who identifies on the male or masculine end of the gender spectrum.

Non-binary: a person who does not find their gender expression on the binary spectrum of male-female. See Enby.

Othering: view or action that treats a person or group of people as intrinsically different from and alien to oneself.

Penetrative Sexuality: a sexuality that derives pleasure from inserting energy or something physical into the body of another, whether that be their tongue, hand, or phallus.

Power Dynamics: a power dynamic is a way that two people, or groups of people, interact with each other, where one of these sides is more powerful than the other one, whether by design or circumstance.

PP: pillow princess. A feminine presenting woman who is a complete sexual receiver in a butch-femme relationship.

Professional Dominatrix: also, a pro-domme. A woman who dominates people in a professional capacity, sometimes for money or for the exchange of goods/services.

Sexual Bottom: a person who, in a sexual situation, receives.

Sexual Submissive: a person who is not dominant during a sexual exchange and seeks to submit or surrender to the sexually dominant attention of their partner.

Stonebutch (SB): an AFAB person who typically presents as hyper-masculine and has touch-restrictive boundaries regarding their body and sexual exchange.

Stonefemme (SF): an AFAB person who typically presents as hyper-feminine and has touch-restrictive boundaries regarding where and how they touch their partners – typically MOC people – during sex.

Stones: the collective group of AFAB people who exist within the lesbian community, though they desire a queered-heteronormative relationship.

Strap/Strapping/Under-Strap: strapping refers to the act of wearing a dildo/harness combination. For some people, they may strap in social situations for gender-validating purposes, or they may restrict strapping to sexual scenarios. Under-strap refers to manipulating genitalia in a way that mimics traditionally male sex-acts (blowjob, hand-job).

Stud: a stud refers to an AFAB person who presents as masculine. This term grew into popularity in urban and hip-hop cultures and has been claimed by masculine presenting POC (people of color).

Third Gender: third gender or third sex is a concept in which individuals are categorized, either by themselves or by society, as neither man nor woman.

Touch-Me-Not (TMN): a group of AFAB people who have complete touch-restrictive boundaries, sexually for certain, but often outside of sex as well. They rarely, if ever, desire touch, though the boundaries are unique to each person.

Tomboy: (aka tomboi) typically refers to a pre- or adolescent AFAB who exhibits characteristics or behaviors considered typical of a boy. Adults may choose to self-identify as a tomboy to denote their interest in masculine activities, while not necessarily feeling like they are trans-identified or MOC.

Top: someone who penetrates their sexual partner.

Trans: someone who was not born into a body that matches their gender. Not all trans-identified people undergo hormone treatment or surgery.

Transmasculine: an AFAB person whose gender rests on the masculine side of the spectrum.

Touch-Them-Not (TTN): another name for pillow princess, or a woman who has rigid boundaries around touching their partner's genitalia or other body parts.

Two-spirit: an umbrella term for people of Indigenous communities in North America who embody more than one gender or gender expression. Being two-spirited was highly valued within these communities, with many two-spirited people being much revered healers and elders. Their community typically acknowledges that they fulfill a traditional, third-gender, ceremonial role.

Under-Strap Blowjob: the act of performing cunnilingus in a way that makes the experience more male for the receiver.

ABOUT THE AUTHOR

Victoria Anne Darling

Victoria Anna Darling has been a writer, educator, organizer, and beautifier for more than 25 years. She founded San Francisco's Femme Posse, Butch/Femme Salons, Butch/Femme Barter List, and the first-ever Butch Appreciation Day in 2002, which is now an international day. Additionally, she launched the first-ever stonebutch/stonefemme focused Facebook group called "Stone for Stone (Butch/Femme)."

Victoria is single, and, after leaving executive roles, has spent the last five years traveling across 48 of the United States with her rescue dog, Jo. She also traveled to Hawaii, Europe, Mexico, and Cuba several times. She now resides in a 200-year-old farmhouse on 100 acres where she sips tea as she watches the sun and moon rise and set every day, hikes through the cornfields, and finds inspiration for her writings.

⋘⋙

If you would like to be added to the author's email list to learn of new books as they are published, please send your name and any comments or feedback to: StoneProudAuthor@gmail.com.

Additional books currently available by this author:

A Stone's Throw: Inside the Stonefemme and Stonebutch Life

The Stone Shelter: A Stonebutch/Stonefemme Love Affair

I Believe in Me! (A fully illustrated children's book on self-selecting pronouns, gender identity, gender expression, and sexuality in relaxed and easy ways, as part of daily living.)

Printed in Great Britain
by Amazon